"She just wants some milk," said
Mrs Green.

3

But the milk jug was empty.

Mr and Mrs Green's cat was hungry.

1

"Stop that noise!" said Mr Green.

Miaow!

2

"I will go and milk the cow," said
Mrs Green.

But the cow would not give any milk.

"She's hungry too," said Mrs Green.

Mrs Green went to get some hay for the cow.

But she could not open the shed. She needed a key.

"Give me the key to the shed," said
Mrs Green to Mr Green.

But Mr Green said, "I can't. I dropped it in the snow."

"Go and dig the key out of the snow," said Mrs Green.

But Mr Green said, "My feet will freeze. My socks have holes in them."

"I will mend your socks," said Mrs Green. But she could not find any wool.

"I will get some wool from the sheep," said Mrs Green. But the sheep would not stand still.

There were too many mice running around. "I will get the cat to chase the mice away," said Mrs Green.

So Mrs Green got the cat.

The cat chased the mice. The sheep stood still.

Mrs Green got some wool. She mended Mr Green's socks.

Mr Green dug in the snow. He found the key to the shed.

Mrs Green got the hay.

Mrs Green fed the cow. The cow gave her some milk.

"Now I can feed the cat," said
Mrs Green.

But the cat was asleep!